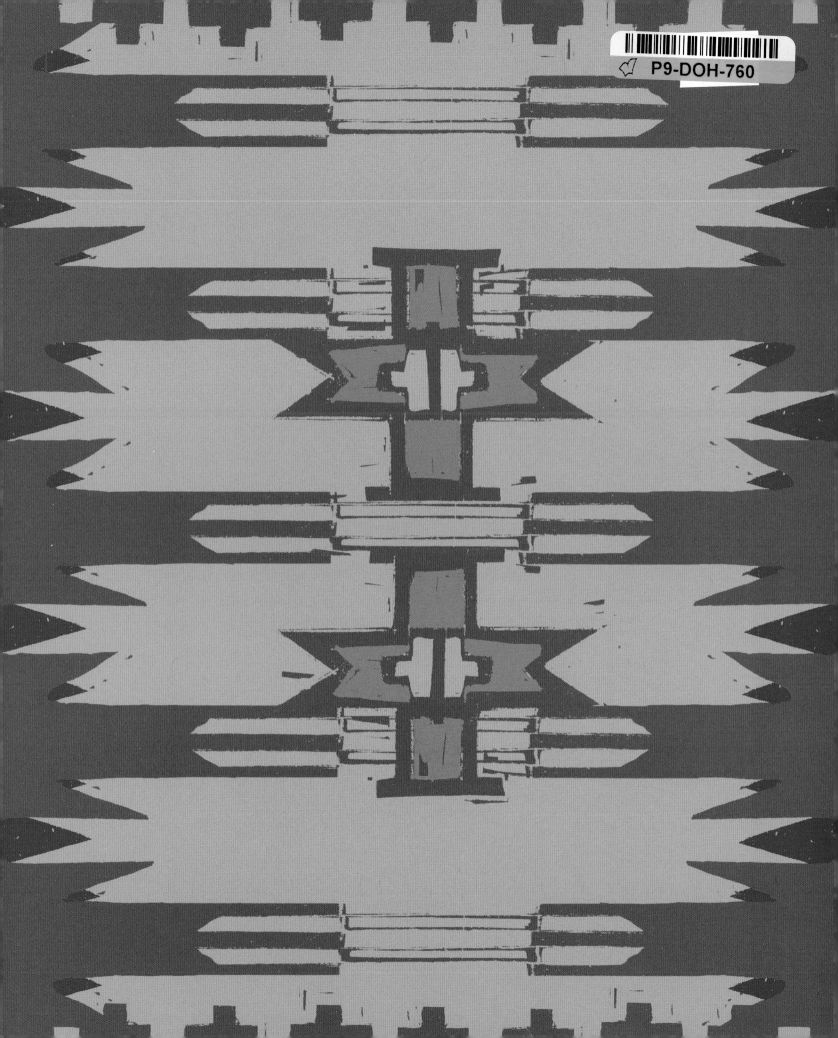

Navajo Long Walk

Navajo

LONG WALK

THE TRAGIC STORY OF A PROUD PEOPLE'S FORCED MARCH FROM THEIR HOMELAND

by

JOSEPH BRUCHAC

Illustrations and captions by

SHONTO BEGAY

NATIONAL GEOGRAPHIC SOCIETY

WASHINGTON, D.C.

For our Grandparents
and for all those who remember — JB

I humbly release my visions in memory of those who sacrificed
and of those who still suffer the aftershocks of these atrocities.
Stay strong, stay Dineh. To the youths of our nation:
Never forget. Do not sacrifice compassion. — SB

I could not have written this book without the help, guidance, and wisdom
of a great many people of the Navajo nation. Such people as Wilson Hunter, Rex Lee Jim,
Shonto Begay, Laura Tohe, Nia Francisco, and Luci Tapahonso have shared
and strengthened Navajo culture through their good work and powerful words.
Foremost among those I must thank is Harry Walters.
His dedication to the true stories of his people is a powerful inspiration for us all. —JB

Published by the National Geographic Society.
All rights reserved. Reproduction of the whole or any part of the contents without written
permission from the National Geographic Society is strictly prohibited.

Book design by LeSales Dunworth.
Shonto Begay's full-color illustrations for this book are acrylic on clay board. His duotone illustrations are watercolor on paper.
Decorative illustrations by Jeffrey Thompson are done on scratch board and colored using a computer.
Text for this book is set in New Century Schoolbook; the display types are Mrs. Eaves and Eagle-Book.
Map by Carl Mehler, Director of Maps; map research and production by XNR Productions.

Library of Congress Cataloging-in-Publication Data
Bruchac, Joseph, 1942–
Navajo long walk / by Joseph Bruchac ; with illustrations by Shonto Begay.
p.   cm.
ISBN 0-7922-7058-4 (hardcover)
1. Navajo Long Walk, 1863–1867. 2. Bosque Redondo Indian Reservation (N.M.).
3. Navajo Indians—History. I. Begay, Shonto, ill. II. Title.

E99.N3 B744 2002
979.1'004972—dc21
2001000567

Printed in China
09/RRDS/4

We were given two ears so that we may hear both sides of every story. One of the tragedies of 19th-century America is that the United States government turned a deaf ear to such native peoples as the Navajos. They wished to live in peace and harmony, but their story went unheard, and their ways were misunderstood. The result was brutal war and forced removal from Dinetah, the beloved Navajo homeland. Yet their tale did not end in defeat. Because of their courage and endurance, and because white Americans finally began to listen, the Navajos regained much of their land. Today, they are the largest tribal nation in the United States. The Navajo Long Walk is an epic of tragedy and triumph all Americans should know.

— **Joseph Bruchac**

The forced removal of the Navajos from our homeland in the 1860s is one of the greatest and least known injustices in American history. Figures such as Kit Carson and General Carleton have been made heroes. In reality they were perpetrators of cultural genocide of the Navajo people and other tribes in the Southwest. Tribes who were friendly and inter-dependent were made enemies or were forced to work against each other. It was a time of great upheaval and of difficult changes that has traumatized a whole nation for generations. Our grandfathers and grandmothers were the walking wounded, and we have inherited a lot of their traumas. Others who experienced similar hardships at the hand of the American government have been recognized for their pain, but the government has never apologized to the Navajo people or made compensation of any kind. The treaties have yet to be honored in full. The collective pain will continue until it is known and recognized. To create the artwork in this book, I had to reach back and gently touch my elders' experience. It reflects great reverence for and consciousness of the pain that they endured and gives homage to their strength, perseverance, and resilience.

— **Shonto Begay**

The coyote foresees the hardship and death that lie ahead for the Navajos. The monochromatic color scheme emphasizes the darkness of this terrible time.—SB

CHAPTER 1

BROKEN CIRCLE

It is a winter day in Canyon de Chelly in 1864. The scene is a peaceful circle of Navajo hogans. Below Navajo Fortress Rock, an old man is about to tell one of the old stories of Coyote that can be told only after the third snowfall of the winter. Suddenly a rider is heard outside and then the warning call: "It is *Bi'éé'lichíí'ii!* Red Clothes and his soldiers are coming. Our enemies the Utes are leading him. We must run."

With those words that circle of peace is broken, perhaps never to be mended again. As the people seek refuge, driving their sheep and goats before them, they look back to see plumes of smoke rising like tall, gray feathers into the air. Their hogans and their stores of corn, dried beans, and squash are burning. Ahead of them they hear the sound of gunfire, and they know that they have been cut off from escape. They scramble

up the walls of the canyon, leaving their animals behind them. Though they have escaped with their lives, they have no food, and the winter winds are cold. One night passes and then another, as they keep moving to avoid the soldiers. The children are shivering from cold, and soon they will be weak from hunger. At last, they realize there is no escape. They fear the soldiers and their Indian allies, Utes who would not hesitate to shoot them like deer. But they have no choice. To survive, they surrender, even though they know what the new soldier chief, Carleton, plans for all the Navajos. They will be taken far away from their beloved homeland to a distant place called the Bosque Redondo.

The Navajo way has always been to seek the path of balance and beauty. Yet now it appears that the only road before them will be a trail of suffering and loss. How did this come to be?

CHAPTER 2

THE GLITTERING WORLD

This land had been the home of the Navajos for countless generations. The Navajo creation story tells how their sacred ancestors, including First Man, First Woman, Coyote, and others of those powerful first beings known as the Holy People, emerged from a hole in the Earth into this world. Its brightness gave it the name Glittering World.

Just after the Emergence, these Holy People decided to build sacred mountains like those that had existed in the previous world. So four mountains were made from four sacred objects. To the east First Woman threw a white shell. Where it landed was created *Sisnaajiní* (Mount Blanca in Colorado), decorated with white shells, white lightning, white corn, dark cloud, and male rain. Next, First Woman threw a turquoise stone. Where it landed in the south they placed *Tsoodził* (Mount Taylor

near Grants, New Mexico), adorned with turquoise, dark mist, female rain, and different kinds of game animals. A piece of abalone landed in the west, and there arose *Dook'o'oosłííd* (the San Francisco Peaks north of Flagstaff, Arizona). Finally, First Woman threw a piece of jet to the north. It marked the site of *Dibe' Nitsaa* (Hesperus Peak in Colorado), which was made beautiful with black beads, dark mist, many kinds of plants, and many wild animals. So it was that the sacred boundaries of the Navajo homeland were set upon the face of the Earth.

The four sacred mountains are the posts of an immense hogan. The hogan is the traditional Navajo home. More than just a place to live, the hogan is a symbolic universe, containing all the things needed to survive. The earth floor of the hogan is Mother Earth herself. The arc of the hogan's roof is the great arch of the Father Sky. Within the center of the hogan is the sacred fire, a source of warmth and life like the sun in the sky.

My version of our creation story illustrates how we are placed in Dinetah—the holy space within the four sacred mountains—and blessed by the rainbow.—SB

The Navajo call themselves *Diné.* It is a word that means "the People." Their sacred homeland is called *Dinetah.* As long as they could remain in Dinetah, in that great hogan among their beloved sacred mountains, the lives of the Navajo people would be blessed. They would walk in the way of *ho'zho,* a Navajo word for the harmony that comes when all living things are in balance. Good fortune and happiness naturally follow. It is this harmony that the soldiers destroyed when they drove the People from Canyon de Chelly.

Red Clothes and his soldiers were not the first men with guns to invade Dinetah. In 1540, the Spanish arrived. The conquistador Francisco Vásquez de Coronado led an expedition of 300 soldiers and 900 Indian servants and slaves into the Southwest searching for Cíbola, with its legendary seven cities of gold. Coronado found no gold, but he left behind the bitter memory of how badly the Spanish treated native people. The Spanish also brought with them a thousand horses and hundreds of sheep and goats. These were the first domestic animals ever seen by the native peoples of the Southwest. These animals changed the Navajos' way of life.

The first Navajos had been hunters and gatherers. Then, from the Pueblo peoples they learned agriculture—how to grow corn, beans, and squash. Indeed, the name "Navajo" is derived from the Tewa Pueblo word *Nabaju,* which means "people with planted fields." With the introduction of sheep, goats, and horses, the Navajos began to build a whole new way of life around their beloved animals.

In 1598, when the Spanish began colonizing the area that would become New Mexico, the Navajos were already skilled herders. Unlike the Pueblos, who were forced to work for the Spanish and who were punished severely by their iron-handed rulers for even the smallest offenses, the Navajos did not live in fixed settlements. They lived in scattered *rancherias,* where they raised their animals. The Spanish frequently attacked the rancherias to take slaves. In retaliation, small parties of Navajos began to raid Spanish settlements for livestock and

to take captives. These captives could be adopted to take the place of Navajos killed or enslaved by the Spanish, or they could be ransomed.

Soon the practice of raid and counter-raid became an established way of life. Whenever a sizable Spanish army was sent against them, the Navajos avoided defeat by retreating into the hills and canyons. Although the Spanish controlled the immediate area around their own towns, the Navajos were the true lords of the land.

Far fewer New Mexicans were taken captive by the Navajos than Navajos were taken captive by the New Mexicans, yet it was the Navajos who became feared as raiders. Most Navajos longed for peace. Time and again they sent peace delegations to Santa Fe, but each time a peace was agreed upon, it was broken by slave raids on the Navajos. The New Mexicans also encouraged the Pueblos to make war on the Navajos and even persuaded a group of Navajos to turn against their own people, promising them wealth and security if they did.

These Navajos from the Cebolleta area became known as the *Diné Ana'í,* or Enemy Navajos. They were led by an ambitious, intelligent, and ruthless Navajo man named Antonio Sandoval. The Enemy Navajos were feared as slave raiders and later as scouts for the U.S. Army. It was not easy for Navajos to escape from their own people, who knew the language and the land.

CHAPTER 3

THE NEW MEN

In early August 1846, an event occurred that would forever change the lives of the Navajo people. The U.S. Army, led by Brigadier General Stephen Watts Kearny, entered Santa Fe. The United States had just fought a one-sided war with Mexico. The territory of New Mexico now became part of the United States by right of conquest. On August 18, General Kearny officially declared control over the citizens of New Mexico, including all of the Indian tribes within the territory.

The Navajos called the Americans the New Men. They hoped to find a peaceful way to exist with them. Had the Americans tried to understand the Navajos, things might have gone very differently. However, the established U.S. policy of dealing with Indians was built not on understanding but on treaties favorable to the United States and

on the use of military power to enforce those agreements. If white settlers wanted Indian land, then the Indians would be removed.

Even after the coming of the Americans, the New Mexicans continued to raid Navajo rancherias for slaves. Navajo children could be sold for as much as $200 each, and it was very common for a New Mexican to own several Navajo slaves. When the Navajos complained to the Americans and asked that their people be freed from slavery, nothing was done. But when the New Mexicans complained of Navajo raids, the U.S. Army quickly took the field against the Indians.

Like the Spanish and the New Mexicans, the Americans also failed to understand that the Navajos were not a single nation with one chief who could speak for everyone. Instead, the Navajos consisted of many bands, each with its own headmen. An agreement with one headman was not binding on all Navajos.

Over the next 16 years, a number of treaties were made between the United States and Navajo headmen. The first of these was the Treaty of Ojo del Oso, signed on October 22, 1846. An elderly and influential headman named Narbona had spoken strongly for peace. So, about 500 Navajos came to the grassy valley of Ojo del Oso, which had natural springs that were held sacred by the Navajos. At that meeting the American in charge, Colonel Alexander W. Doniphan, told the Navajos that if they did not stop their raids, the United States would make war on them. The Navajos thought this was a strange demand. The Americans were fighting a war against other Americans who held slaves. Should not the New Men be the Navajos' allies against the New Mexican slave raiders? Zarcillos Largos, another Navajo headman, spoke for his people:

> *Americans! You have a strange cause for war against the Navajos. We have waged war against the New Mexicans for many years. We have plundered their villages and killed many of their people.*

> *You have lately commenced a war against the same people. You are powerful. You have great guns and many brave soldiers. You have therefore conquered them, the very same thing we have been attempting to do for so many years.*

You now turn upon us for attempting what you have done yourselves.
We cannot see why you have cause to quarrel with us for fighting the
New Mexicans on the west, while you do the same on the east.

Despite his uncertainty, Zarcillos Largos and ten other Navajo headmen signed that first peace treaty between the United States and the Navajo people. Unfortunately, the trade in Navajo slaves did not cease. If anything, it increased in the years that followed.

Three years later, Narbona attended another treaty-making meeting with a party of New Mexican volunteers and American soldiers. It took place at Washington Pass on the north fork of Tunicha Creek near the present-day Two Grey Hills trading post. Narbona was now well over 80 years old, but his people still listened to him when he urged them to live in peace. Colonel J. M. Washington was discussing the proposed treaty with the old man when a New Mexican accused one of the Navajos of riding a horse that had been stolen from him. The soldiers immediately tried to seize the Navajo. When he and his friends tried to escape, the soldiers opened fire on all of the Navajos. Six Navajos were killed, including Narbona, whose long white hair was ripped from his

My painting shows more than the death of Narbona. The wet ink on the treaty is symbolic of a disrupted peace—something that is ongoing.—SB

head by a New Mexican scalp hunter. A few Navajos eventually signed the Treaty of Washington Pass, but the murder of Narbona had killed any chance for a meaningful peace agreement.

Even though they now distrusted the Americans, many Navajos still tried to find ways to live with them in peace. It was hard for the Americans to decide on a firm policy for dealing with the Indians because the Indian agents and governors in Santa Fe changed so rapidly. The best of the many Indian agents was a man named Henry L. Dodge, appointed in May 1853. He was the first agent to actually live among the Navajos. He always treated them with respect and honesty and tried to act in their best interests. He hired a blacksmith and a silversmith to teach new and useful trades to the Navajos, who quickly became creative metalworkers, transforming silver coins into necklaces and other jewelry. The Navajos grew to love Dodge during his two years in office. They called him *Bi'éé'łichíí'ii,* Red Shirt, for the red flannel shirts he always wore. Had Dodge remained as Indian agent, the later wars between the United States and the Navajos might never have happened. But in 1855 while he was out hunting deer with a group of Navajo friends, he became separated from the others and was killed by a party of Apaches.

The Navajos were not blamed for Dodge's death, but they had lost their best advocate. More treaties were signed, taking the best land for grazing away from the Navajos and making it hard for them to maintain their herds. Forts were built or reinforced to keep the Navajos out of the lands that had always been theirs.

In the summer of 1858, because of a severe drought, the Navajos returned their herds to some of that land near Fort Defiance. When soldiers from the fort found the animals grazing there, they opened fire, killing about 48 cattle that belonged to a Navajo headman named Manuelito. Many Navajos now felt certain that unless they went on raids for food they would starve. The hostilities that followed were ended by the Bonneville Treaty of December 1858. This treaty, however, was meant to punish the Navajos, and it took away even more of their land.

Finally, the Navajos could stand it no longer. In 1860, a large force of Navajos, led by Manuelito, attacked Fort Defiance in an attempt to reclaim traditional grazing lands. Although the attack failed, the Army recognized how desperate the Navajos had become. Colonel Edward S. Canby, who had led the recent campaign, convinced 47 Navajo headmen to sign a treaty. The Canby Treaty of 1861 led to a new approach to encourage the Navajos to stop raiding. In February 1861 the Army began a successful policy of issuing rations to the Navajos at places such as Fort Fauntleroy. In April of that same year, the American Civil War began. Although that conflict was between the Americans of the North and the South, it would soon deeply involve the Navajos and bring about the most tragic events in their history. The brief truce that had brought peace to the canyons of Dinetah would soon be broken by the thunder of white men's guns.

CHAPTER 4

THE FEARING TIME

The New Mexico Territory was in the path of a Southern army moving north and west from Texas to take control of gold fields in California. The American soldiers—among them a former mountain man named Kit Carson—were pulled from the forts to meet the Confederate threat. It meant the end of the policy of providing rations to the hungry Navajos. Before long, many Navajos felt they had no choice but to return to raiding to survive.

The Confederate plan failed. The Southern forces were defeated at Glorieta Pass, and the threat of invasion ended. General James H. Carleton, the new military commander of the New Mexico Territory, looked around for a new enemy. He decided on the Navajos and the Apaches. The New Mexicans told him that these Indians were lawless raiders. Like so many others before him, he did not listen to the native side of the story. He decided to crush them in battle and then remove them from their lands.

Carleton knew just the man to lead his campaign—Kit Carson, who was now a colonel. The Navajos called him Red Clothes and Rope Thrower. Carson had a reputation as an Indian fighter. Carleton sent him first against the Mescalero Apaches, who numbered fewer than the Navajos. Within a few months, by constantly pursuing the Mescaleros and burning their homes and crops, Carson had defeated them. The Mescaleros were shipped to a place known as the Bosque Redondo, or Round Grove. Despite its name, which came from the cottonwood trees scattered along the Pecos River, it was a barren place in the salt flats of eastern New Mexico. A new military outpost named Fort Sumner was built there to guard the Indian prisoners. The location was Carleton's choice, even though there was poor water, little firewood, and bad soil. Others in the military tried to change his mind, arguing that the site

was not the best choice. Carleton was adamant. He would make the Bosque Redondo a model reservation, his own "Fair Carletonia." It was there that Carleton planned to send the Navajos.

The Navajos tried to talk with Carleton. A delegation of 18 headmen led by Barboncito and Delgadito, two well-known and respected Navajo leaders, tried to arrange a truce. General Carleton refused to talk to them. "We have no faith in their promises," Carleton said, ignoring the fact that little if any promise-breaking had been done by the Navajos.

In 1863, using Ute Indians for his scouts, Kit Carson took the field against the Navajos. The Utes were traditional enemies of the Navajos and often captured Navajos to sell. Carson suggested that part of the Utes' payment could be Navajo slaves. The time the Navajos call *Nidahadzid daa,* the "Fearing Time," had begun.

General Carleton issued his brutal orders to Kit Carson: "Say to them: Go to the Bosque Redondo or we will pursue and destroy you. We will not make peace with you on any other terms."

Carson was to pursue them, not with a large army but with "small parties moving stealthily to their haunts," until they could fight no more. Carleton did not hate the Navajos, but he also did not seem to view them as human beings. "An Indian," he wrote, "is more watchful and wary an animal than a deer. He must be hunted with skill. . . ."

Once again, the Navajos sent a delegation pleading for peace. Only a few of us have raided, they said. Most of us are peaceful people. We have not broken the treaties. As before, they were ignored. As the military campaign continued, any Navajos found by the Army were shot on sight unless they immediately surrendered. Many stories about that time of being hunted by the white soldiers and their Indian scouts are still remembered by the Navajos. One tells of a man who escaped the Army by jumping off a high cliff. His fall was broken by the bushes and treetops below, and he escaped unharmed.

Most Navajos did not understand why they were being rounded up. Some thought they were being removed so that white people could have

their land. Others heard that they were being taken to a place where they would all be put to death. Although some Navajos never were caught, seeking refuge in such rough areas as the lands around Navajo Mountain, most of the people had no other choice. They could starve, be shot, or be taken as slaves—or they could surrender to the Army. With dignity and great sorrow, Delgadito led 200 members of his band in to surrender in 1863. Other headmen followed as Carson's campaign became more intense.

Carson's armies were cutting through the heart of Dinetah like a sharp blade through corn. All of the Navajos' old enemies were against them. There was no place to hide. Even Canyon de Chelly was not safe.

Following pages: Sacred corn pollen, symbol of new generations, is trampled by horses' hooves as soldiers storm Canyon de Chelly. The lightning suggests harmony being destroyed.—SB

In January 1864, Carson marched into this ancient refuge, and the people fled. The hogans in the canyon were burned, and the thousands of peach trees they had lovingly tended were cut down.

Desperate, hungry Navajo families now flocked to the newly named Fort Canby (which originally had been called Fort Defiance and which would revert to its old name again after 1864). The weak and suffering Navajos were then taken from Fort Canby to the staging area at Fort Wingate. From there, long columns of Navajo prisoners would be forced to walk east toward Fort Sumner under harsh military escort. Even Manuelito, the great war leader who had planned the attack on Fort Defiance, eventually came in with his people—though he did not do so until 1866.

Soon the staging areas at the forts held as many Indians as they could handle. The military campaign against the Navajos ended. But the terrible ordeal was not over yet.

The Long Walk east to Fort Sumner and the Bosque Redondo was about to begin.

CHAPTER 5

THE WALK ITSELF

It is more than 470 hard miles from Fort Canby to Fort Sumner. This is
the distance that was walked by all the Navajos who were driven from
their homeland. Today, U.S. Route 40 follows the same trail the struggling
Navajos were forced to march upon. It runs past Gallup, New Mexico,
over the dark lava flow said to be the blood of a monster killed long ago
by the Navajo Hero Twins. It leads below the cliffs and mesas of Acoma
and Laguna, where the Pueblo people watched the long lines of Navajos
trudging wearily past. It passes under the shade of the great Sandia
Crest near Albuquerque and then rolls on across land that is drier and
flatter and more and more barren with each mile. This was the trail
that brought the suffering people closer to their destination. It is a
journey that, in a car today, is by turns strikingly picturesque and

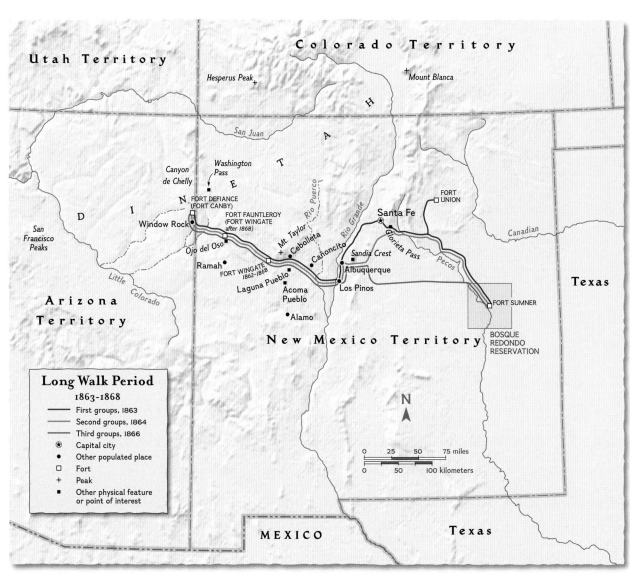

Utah Territory

Colorado Territory

Hesperus Peak +

+ Mount Blanca

San Juan

Canyon
de Chelly

Washington
Pass

San
Francisco
Peaks

N A V A J O

D I N E T A H

FORT DEFIANCE
(FORT CANBY)

FORT FAUNTLEROY
(FORT WINGATE
after 1868)

Window Rock

Ojo del Oso

Ramah

FORT WINGATE
1862-1868

Little Colorado

Rio Puerco

Mt. Taylor
Cebolleta

Cañoncito

Rio Grande

Santa Fe

FORT
UNION

Glorieta Pass

Pecos

Canadian

Sandia Crest

Albuquerque

Laguna Pueblo

Acoma
Pueblo

Los Pinos

Alamo

Arizona
Territory

New Mexico Territory

FORT SUMNER

BOSQUE
REDONDO
RESERVATION

Texas

Long Walk Period

1863-1868

—— First groups, 1863
—— Second groups, 1864
—— Third groups, 1866
⊛ Capital city
● Other populated place
☐ Fort
+ Peak
■ Other physical feature
   or point of interest

N

0   25   50   75 miles

0   50   100 kilometers

MEXICO

Texas

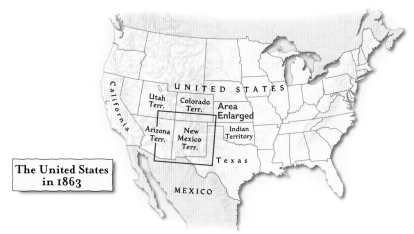

UNITED STATES

California

Utah
Terr.

Colorado
Terr.

Area
Enlarged

Arizona
Terr.

New
Mexico
Terr.

Indian
Territory

Texas

MEXICO

The United States
in 1863

then monotonous. Neither of those words, however, can describe the experience it was for the suffering Navajos.

There was, in fact, more than one Long Walk. Parties of Navajos of various sizes set out from Fort Canby and Fort Wingate over a three-year period. Even before the Long Walk began in force in 1864, about 200 Navajo forced emigrants were led to the Bosque Redondo by the headman Delgadito in November 1863. Later parties would be much larger.

At first, all of the captive Navajos were forced to make a long detour off the route to Santa Fe, 60 miles north. It was Carleton's orders that the once fierce Navajos should be paraded down the narrow, winding streets of the capital city to be displayed to the citizens as helpless, defeated prisoners. Later in 1864, when the number of Navajos grew too large, this detour to Santa Fe was abandoned. For a time, though no one knows why, the route detoured 70 miles farther north to Fort Union.

Although the Army had orders to use wagons, horses, and mules to help carry the sick, the children, and the crippled, they were seldom used for this purpose. The soldiers rode and the Indians walked. Anyone too weak or too ill to keep up would be shot or left behind. The late Howard Gorman, a deeply respected elder whose ancestors made that terrible journey, told a story passed down to him by his elders.

Following pages: Images of a forced relocation—the cries of children, moans of the dying, futile prayers uttered in the snow and mud along a blood-soaked trail—were emotionally difficult to recreate.—SB

Somewhere near *K'aałogii Dził,* Butterfly Mountain, south of Albuquerque, a young woman who was about to give birth could keep up no longer. Her relatives begged the soldiers to wait for her. They were forced to move on. One soldier rode back. Then the sound of a gunshot was heard.

Some of the columns of Navajos stretched for five miles across the wide land. They could average no more than ten or twelve miles a day, and the weather was often harsh as they traveled. They slept outside with no shelters or blankets. Some had livestock that they drove along with them, but Ute Indian raiders and New Mexican slavers attacked the columns, driving off animals and taking prisoners. The Navajos were not well fed, and the food they were given was sometimes strange to them. At Fort Canby, where they were held before setting out, they were given coffee beans. The Navajos, who thought they were like pinto beans, boiled the coffee beans and tried to eat them. Given white flour rather than the cornmeal they were used to, the Navajos tried to eat it raw or mix it with water to make a thin soup. As a result, they became sick. Between February 20 and March 6, 1864, 126 Navajos died of dysentery at Fort Canby.

Perhaps the most tragic of the Long Walks was the one that began on March 4, 1864, with 2,150 Navajos. It was the largest group to set out, and the number increased to more than 2,500 as they traveled. Though they were weakened by their encampment at Fort Canby and harried along the march by New Mexican raiders, their worst enemy would prove to be the weather. General Carleton himself made note of it, writing, "The weather was very inclement, with terrible gales of wind and heavy snow. The Indians were nearly naked; and, besides, many died from dysentery occasioned from eating too heartily of half cooked bread made from our flour, to which they were not accustomed."

Perhaps one in every ten of the people who set out on that trip died along the way, their frozen bodies marking the trail.

As the roundup of Navajos continued, it became clear to General Carleton that he had miscalculated. Carleton had originally estimated that there were no more than 8,000 Navajos. But by November 1864, 8,750 men, women, and children were counted at Fort Sumner. Ironically, this number included even the Diné Ana'í, the Enemy Navajos, who had long fought their own people and had allied themselves with the New Mexicans. In Carleton's eyes, it did not matter that at one time they had helped the Army. All that mattered was that they were Navajos. However, so many hungry and poor people, the largest concentration of Indians on the North American continent, stretched the resources of the

Army to the breaking point. There was not enough food or necessities at Fort Sumner. No more Indians could be brought by the Army to Bosque Redondo. The Long Walks ended. Military operations out of Fort Wingate against the Navajos ended in the spring and summer of 1865. As a result, several thousand Navajos remained in their homeland, hiding in the most desolate places from armed New Mexicans who had been urged by General Carleton to "kill all the Navajo men who run away from the Bosque or who will not go there."

Meanwhile, the Navajos who were now held at the Bosque wondered how they would survive. They called their place of captivity *Hwééldi,* from the Spanish word *fuerte,* meaning "strong place." Some Navajos said it meant "Place of the Wind," for only the wind—which did not need to eat or drink—could live there.

CHAPTER 6

THE BOSQUE REDONDO

Like many of the military men of his time, General Carleton believed
it was his job to "kill the Indian and save the man." By giving them
civilization, he would make life better for the Navajos. Thus, life for his
Indians at the Bosque Redondo was supposed to be a paradise on Earth.
But that paradise existed only in Carleton's mind. Ignoring the hard
facts that faced him, he sent back glowing reports of life at Fair Carletonia.
It was a place where the Apache and Navajo prisoners would be weaned
from their old ways. There, as Carleton wrote, the Army "will be kind to
them; there teach their children to read and write; teach them the arts
of peace. Soon they would acquire new habits, new ideas, new modes of
life; the old Indians . . . would die off, and carry with them all the latent
longings for murdering and robbing."

From the very start, Carletonia was a dismal failure. The reservation was 40 miles by 40 miles. It was based on Carleton's very poorly thought out recommendations and was established by an order from President Abraham Lincoln on January 15, 1864. The very fact that 400 Mescalero Apaches and more than 8,000 Navajos were confined to a single reservation was itself a mistake. Though cousins, the two native nations had fought each other in the past, and they resented being forced to share the same reservation. Eventually, the entire Mescalero Apache population escaped from the Bosque, leaving the Navajos behind.

"The Bosque," Carleton had written in 1863, "was the best pastoral region between the two oceans. Within ten years the Navajos would be the happiest and most delightfully located pueblo of Indians in New Mexico, perhaps in the United States."

It soon became evident to everyone except the general that his plan to make Bosque Redondo a garden spot was doomed. The first year's corn crop, planted in the dry, alkaline soil and weakened by a severe winter, failed. The second year's corn crop also failed, as did the third and the fourth. Carleton persisted, ordering the Navajos to work in the fields even when the weather was extremely bad. In February 1865, a hundred Navajos, forced to plow the fields in the midst of a blizzard, froze to death.

Carleton had tried to make the Navajos live in one single pueblo-style village. The Navajos refused. They preferred the old ways of separating into smaller bands and following their own headmen.

Carleton finally gave in. He was the first American military leader to accept what the Navajos had told everyone all along: They were not one unified tribe but a number of bands, each with its own headmen. The General appointed Kit Carson to help set up ten separate towns on the Bosque, each with its own headmen.

But even this reorganization on something like a traditional model was not enough to really help the lives of the Navajos who were held prisoner there. The rations were hardly ever enough for the people. The Army bought additional supplies from civilian contractors, but the food sent to the Indians was often spoiled or contaminated with rat droppings. There was little firewood. Although the Army forced the Navajos to build barracks for the soldiers, the Indians lived first in holes they dug in the ground and then in rough hogans made of brush and mud and whatever else they could find. What few livestock the Navajos had managed to keep were not safe. The Kiowas and Comanches made regular raids on the Bosque, striking so swiftly that the soldiers in the fort could seldom respond in time.

The Navajos could not understand why they were being punished this way. As Howard Gorman explained in *Navajo Stories of the Long Walk Period,* "They said among themselves, 'What did we do wrong? We people here didn't do any harm. The ones that were doing all the killing and raiding of the White Men probably are still doing the same thing back home.... We harmless people are held here, and we want to go back to our homes right away.'"

I can feel the cold chill in the bones of these battered and subdued people living on the brink of nonexistence. Their faith gives them strength to endure.—SB

Soon, Navajos began to follow the lead of the Apaches and slip away from Hwééldi. Carleton issued orders that any Navajo caught away from the reservation without one of the metal passes made by the fort's blacksmiths would be shot. Before long, counterfeit metal passes made by Navajo metalworkers were more common than the real ones. By 1865, large numbers of Navajos were escaping from the reservation and making their way back to Dinetah. Some were raiding the ranches near Fort Sumner or striking back against the Comanches and Kiowas. Meanwhile, the Army was finding it harder and harder to feed and care for its unwilling charges. The 40 miles square of the Bosque Redondo held not only the largest single concentration of Indians in the United States but also the unhappiest.

THE WALK HOME

Life for the Navajos at Bosque Redondo grew worse every year. They only received food every other day. The medicines given them were bad, the blankets so poorly made that Navajo women unraveled them to weave them again. There was so little firewood that everyone was always cold. Their small herds of livestock continued to decline.

By 1865, General Carleton was asking the Indian Service of the Department of the Interior to take over the reservation. The Army was not being given enough money by Congress to take care of the almost 8,000 Navajos who still remained at the Bosque. The Superintendent of Indian Affairs refused. The Army had rounded up the Navajos and placed them at Fort Sumner. It was the Army's job to care for them.

Word of the awful conditions at the Bosque spread. The American

Civil War, which would end in May 1865, was drawing to a close. Congress was now free to turn its attention to the plight of the Navajos. It was vitally important to find solutions for the various conflicts between American settlers and the western Indians whose lands they were occupying. The plight of the Navajos at the Bosque Redondo became a much publicized controversy. In June 1865, a congressional delegation, the Doolittle Committee, held hearings at Fort Sumner. One of those questioned was the Navajo headman Herrero. "The soldiers about here treat us very bad," Herrero said, "whipping and kicking us." The congressmen listened to the Navajos. For the first time, the real cause of the Navajo wars—the generations of slave raids against the Indians—was discovered. Despite these findings, no real action was taken to help the Navajos at the Bosque.

However, public and congressional opposition to General Carleton's dictatorial rule increased. Charges of fraud and mismanagement grew. Finally, on April 2, 1867, Carleton was removed from command of the New Mexico District. The Department of the Interior's Indian Service took control of Bosque Redondo. Almost immediately, the Indian Service recommended the reservation be closed.

The question now was what to do with the Navajos. Some wanted to return them to a small reservation that would be established in their old homeland. Others opposed that. One reason for removing the Navajo had been to allow white people to seek valuable minerals. Although no gold or silver had been discovered yet in Dinetah, no one knew what might be found in the future. So, they suggested sending the Navajo people east to Indian Territory in what is now Oklahoma. Herrero had already stated what the Navajos wanted. "All the Navajos," he said, "longed to return to their lofty mesas and red sand country."

In April 1868, several Navajo headmen, including Manuelito and Barboncito, were brought to Washington to meet with President Andrew Johnson. It was decided that a Peace Commission would be sent to New Mexico to decide the future of the Navajo people. When the Navajo leaders returned to the Bosque, they held a sacred ceremony involving a coyote that was captured and then released in a circle of Navajos. Coyote is one of the Navajo Holy People and holds a deeply sacred place in Navajo belief. The coyote walked slowly out of the circle, heading west toward Dinetah. This was a sign that the people must go home. At that Coyote Ceremony, Barboncito, a deeply spiritual headman, was chosen as chief spokesman for all the Navajos still held in captivity at Fort Sumner.

The Peace Commission was led by General William Tecumseh Sherman, one of the heroes for the North in the Civil War. Although he had a reputation as a ruthless warrior, Sherman was appalled at the suffering the Navajos had endured. "I found the Bosque," he said, "a mere spot of green in the midst of wild desert, and the Navajos had sunk into a condition of absolute poverty and despair."

Barboncito was eloquent and direct with the commission. When asked what the Navajos wanted, he replied, "I hope to God that you will not ask me to go to any other country except my own." Further, he said,

"If we go back to our own country, we are willing to abide by whatever orders are issued to us."

The next day, ten headmen delegated by the Navajos signed what turned out to be the first fair treaty between their people and the United States government. Among them were Herrero, Barboncito, and Manuelito. The Navajos were finally going home. On June 18, 1868, a column of Navajos ten miles long set out from Fort Sumner. With them were 50 supply wagons and four companies of cavalry. The people were so filled with joy that the first sight of Mount Taylor, the easternmost of their sacred peaks, overwhelmed them. "When we saw the top of the mountain from Albuquerque we wondered if it was our mountain and felt like falling to the ground, we

Coyote gently exits the circle, foretelling the Navajos' impending release. The bright light represents the hope that negotiations with the Peace Commission will be successful.—SB

loved it so." One old woman was so moved that she exclaimed, "Sacred mountain, I am home," and then she died. From then on, it is said, the Navajos were careful not to let their elders catch sight of their sacred mountains too quickly for fear their hearts would fail.

Fort Defiance, near Window Rock, Arizona, was the closest Army post to the new reservation. It was set up as the headquarters for the Indian Service's Navajo agent and as a supply depot. It was not easy for the Navajos to rebuild their homes and start again. Their new reservation was very small, but they were home. In 1869, the government began to give them the livestock promised in the treaty: 30,000 sheep and 4,000 goats purchased by the Indian Affairs Office from local ranches in Arizona and New Mexico.

From that point on, the Navajo nation grew. As the number of people and the sizes of their herds increased, the government enlarged the boundaries of the reservation through executive orders. By 1880, the original 3,328,000 acres had doubled. Finally it covered a large part of their original homeland. Although the Diné Ana'í were not mentioned in the Treaty of 1868, they were allowed to return to their homes at Canoncito, in New Mexico, and eventually were granted lands now designated as the Canoncito Navajo Reservation. Two other separate Navajo reservation sites were established in New Mexico at Ramah and Alamo. Although they are detached from the much larger main reservation, those three areas take part in Navajo tribal government. Today, more than 150,000 Navajos live on what has become the largest of all reservations in the United States.

If you look down into Canyon de Chelly, you will see Navajo hogans again. There, at night beside the fire in one of those hogans, an old man tells his grandchildren a story of long ago. Perhaps it is a tale of Creation or of one of the monsters that threatened the lives of the people. It is a story that speaks of the deep connection between the Diné and the sacred land. It is, like the history of the Long Walk, a tale of difficulty, of danger, and of survival that is inspiring to us all.

AFTERWORD

The Navajo people have kept their promise to live in peace with the United States. They have become known as great herders of livestock and deeply gifted silverworkers. The beautiful rugs woven by Navajo women are prized all over the world. Though the Navajos never fought the United States again, their warrior spirit and the urge to defend their sacred land has remained strong. Volunteering to fight in the American armed forces has become a tradition followed by thousands of Navajos. In World War II, Navajo soldiers played an important role. The Japanese were monitoring American communications and had deciphered every American code. Navajo servicemen devised an unbreakable code based on their own language. Soon Navajo code talkers were at the heart of the American Signal Corps, and their efforts contributed greatly to winning the war in the Pacific.